For

Marian —
my "time-honored"
friend Love,
1-18-97   Judy Hoffman

TIME-HONORED
FRIENDS

The Best is Yet to Come

By John P. Beilenson

PETER PAUPER PRESS, INC.
WHITE PLAINS · NEW YORK

Cover Design by Mullen & Katz
Cover photograph ©1994 Jill Sabella,
reprinted with the permission of FPG International.
Design by Michel Design
Photographs by Solomon M. Skolnick

Copyright © 1995
Peter Pauper Press, Inc.
202 Mamaroneck Avenue
White Plains, NY 10601
All rights reserved
ISBN 0-88088-888-1
Printed in Singapore
7 6 5 4 3

Introduction

❦

Grow old along with me!
The best is yet to be . . .

Robert Browning

❦

Old friends are deep sources
of joy. If we are mindful of
our friends, we remain con-
nected to precious memories,
to happy times and places that

remind us of the best parts of who we were, who we are now, and who we are becoming.

∞

Those who find their oldest friends next door or nearby must consider themselves truly blessed. A short drive or a local phone call, and they can find a trusted confidante, a sensitive adviser, a practiced and attentive listener.

*A*s we grow older, we often have more freedom to spend our days as we please. So pack a bag (small or large), grab a good friend (small or large), and set out on some adventure. This is surely one of the secrets of a long and happy life.

∞

*C*ome along with us, and sample some of the wisdom

and wit within. And if something here reminds you of someone near or far, pick up a pen or the phone or make a visit. Share a memory, or better yet remind them: the best is yet to be.

J. P. B.

Laughter
is the golden thread
woven through all
friendships.

$\mathcal{T}$ime heals all wounds . . .
and strengthens all bonds.

❧

$\mathcal{A}$n old friendship is
like a well-worn coat. It fits us
perfectly, keeps us warm, and
shows off our best features.

*P*assions may come and go,
but friendships last a lifetime.

❧

*O*ne can never
have too many books or
too many friends.

9

A good friendship is like a
vintage wine that grows better
as it grows older.

❧

*F*riendship is a
path to those things
that are eternal.

*A long friendship
is a house with many
rooms and with countless
happy memories.*

When we do know
where to turn, we turn to
old friends.
When we don't know
where to turn, we turn to
old friends.

For even the oldest
friendships, each day can
be a new beginning.

❧

The best measure of
our lives is how we treat
our friends.

FRIENDSHIPS ARE
NEVER DESTINATIONS.
THEY ARE JOURNEYS INTO
UNKNOWN PLACES THAT
WE LEARN TO MAKE
OUR OWN.

Old friendships are
like perennial flowers.
They continue to bloom
year after year.

In a world of rapid
change, good friends
are a constant.

Time-honored friends
are the stars by which we
navigate our lives.

❧

Long-standing
friendships are like antiques:
they get more valuable
with age.

An old friend's frown
can be more valuable than a
new friend's smile.

As we get older,
we may misplace our
glasses, but we never
forget our friends.

Like the strings on a well-tuned violin, an old friendship is neither strung too loosely nor too tightly.

The friendships that
last are those that have the
capacity to change.

❧

The laughter of friends
is part of any happy day and
every healthy life.

19

Time-honored friendships
are like aged trees: they have
deep roots, they provide
real shade.

❧

The longer we
travel the road of life,
the more important are our
traveling companions.

It is one of the true
joys of life to do for our
friends without expecting
anything in return.

Time-honored friends
don't volunteer to carry
the stool when the piano
needs moving.

In the end, we
receive no more from
our friends than we risk
giving to them.

❧

Think: what have
you done for an old
friend lately?

True friendship
is simply two hearts
working together to
carry one load.

A life lived
giving to friends is
worth living.

❧

No day is
perfect until you
have done something
for a friend.

When we give flowers
to a friend, the fragrance
lingers on us.

᠅

Time-honored
friendships are the
foundation of a
happy life.

FRIENDS

ARE THE BEST
SHELTER FROM
LIFE'S INEVITABLE
STORMS.

Time-honored
friends will remember your
birthday, but won't remind
you of your age.

❧

Embrace your friends.
Embrace life.

*O*ld friends
hold precious
memories.

❧

*R*eal friendships
give off both light
and heat.

*Friendship is
the glue that keeps our
lives together—especially
when it feels as if
everything is
falling apart.*

If I were to draw a
picture of heaven, there
would be the biggest, bluest
sky you have ever seen, and
all the friends I have
ever known.

Love may have
its day, but friendship
is forever.

❧❦❧

Real friendship
is like a spring in winter;
it never stops flowing.

We are proud
of our grandchildren,
our daughters and sons,
and prouder still of
our friends.

It makes no sense
to save the kind words and
tenderness we have for our
friends. Give them now.
Give them freely.

I would rather have
the company of one true
friend than of all the rulers
in the world.

True friendship grows slowly and often through adversity. That's why time-honored friendship is so strong, why it should be cherished.

There are few
problems that can't be
helped by a conversation
with an old friend.

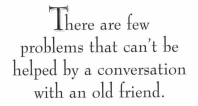

The best thing
about an old friend is
that she knows you . . .
and still loves you.

Rekindled friendships
often burn more brightly.

The longest
friendships can grow
from the humblest
beginnings.

The good life is
not a solo performance;
it is a voice lifted
with others.

⁘

Call an old friend for
no particular reason.

*T*rue friendship is
like a rose. It retains its
beauty if it is well-kept
and cared for.

❧

*L*ife can be hard,
but the strongest friendships
can be forged in our most
difficult moments.

A friend-ship is the world's best ocean liner. It is stable enough for rough waters, and it gets you where you are going in comfort and style.

Each year,
along with your bulbs,
plant the beginnings of
a few new friendships.
That way your life, like
your garden, will always
be full of blooms.

A faithful friend
is a kind housekeeper.
While listening to all your
meandering thoughts, she will
help you straighten up what's
worth keeping, and with a
broom of tenderness
sweep the rest out
the back door.

We are constantly
reminded to save our money
for our old age, but we will
have little of value in our later
years if we don't preserve
our friendships.

❦

Old friendships are
accustomed to taking risks.

We should make
sure to travel often to our
friends' homes; the unused
path soon grows over.

The touch of a friend's
hand—the sound of a friend's
voice—these are life's
greatest presents.

Like a shadow, a false
friend is there only while the
sun is shining. True friends
are there in all weather.

⚜

If we can't afford to
make the gift of friendship,
we will rarely have the
opportunity to
receive it.

As we get older,
it is always exciting to
make a new discovery,
but perhaps the most
thrilling is to find a
new friend.

Old friends bring out
the best in us.

✦

Friendship is
the rosy dawn of any
happy old age.

Two old friends
may appear as if they are
in the Winter of their lives,
but look more closely and
you will find an
indomitable Spring.

Friendships keep the cold winds of pessimism from our souls.

*T*ime-honored
friendships are blessings
showered on us from
on high.

❧

*O*ld friends are
the only true form of
social security.

True friends
live through giving.

❧

Eloquent listening
is the mark of an old,
true friend.

Just as we
have taken time
to choose our friends,
so should we consider
carefully before
changing them.

*The oldest
friendships throw off the
greatest sparks of joy.
Friendship grows strongest
in the soil of simplicity,
goodness, and truth.*

*G*reat friendships
are made from small
acts done with simple
kindness.

❧

*O*ld friendships are
generally made up of two
forgiving people.

*The loyalty
of a time-honored
friendship can never
be breached.*

Friendship is
a golden chain that
binds us one
to another.

❧

Love an old
friend with your eyes,
and see her with
your heart.

Yesterday is
gone. Today can always
get better. Tomorrow is
filled with promise. The
best is yet to be!